FIREFIGHTER

Philip Abraham

HIGH
interest
books

Children's Press®
A Division of Scholastic Inc.
New York / Toronto / London / Auckland / Sydney
Mexico City / New Delhi / Hong Kong
Danbury, Connecticut

Special thanks to Jay G. Bender, Fire Marshal of Fair Lawn, New Jersey.
Special thanks also to the firefighters of Iselin District #11, NJ.

Book Design: Michelle Innes and Mindy Liu
Contributing Editor: Eric Fein

Photo Credits: Cover, pp. 1, 5, 39 © SuperStock, Inc.; pp. 3, 43, 45, 47 © Rubberball
Productions; pp. 7, 35 © George Hall/Corbis; p. 9 © Hulton/Archive/Getty Images;
p. 10 © Index Stock Imagery, Inc.; pp. 12–13 © AP/Wide World Photos; p. 15
© Underwood & Underwood/Corbis; p. 19 © Corbis; p. 21 © Richard T.
Nowitz/Corbis; p. 25 © AFP/Corbis; p. 27 © John M. Roberts/Corbis; pp. 28,
31, 36 Courtesy of Michelle Innes; p. 32 © Photodisc

Library of Congress Cataloging-in-Publication Data

Abraham, Philip, 1970-
    Firefighter / Philip Abraham.
      p. cm. — (Danger is my business)
    Summary: Introduces the type of work, dangers, and requirements for the
    job of firefighter.
    ISBN 0-516-24339-X (lib. bdg.) — ISBN 0-516-27866-5 (pbk.)
    1. Fire extinction—Juvenile literature. 2. Fire fighters—Juvenile
    literature. [1. Fire extinction—Vocational guidance. 2. Fire fighters.
    3. Vocational guidance.] I. Title. II. Series.

TH9148.A26 2003
628.9'25—dc21   2002155012

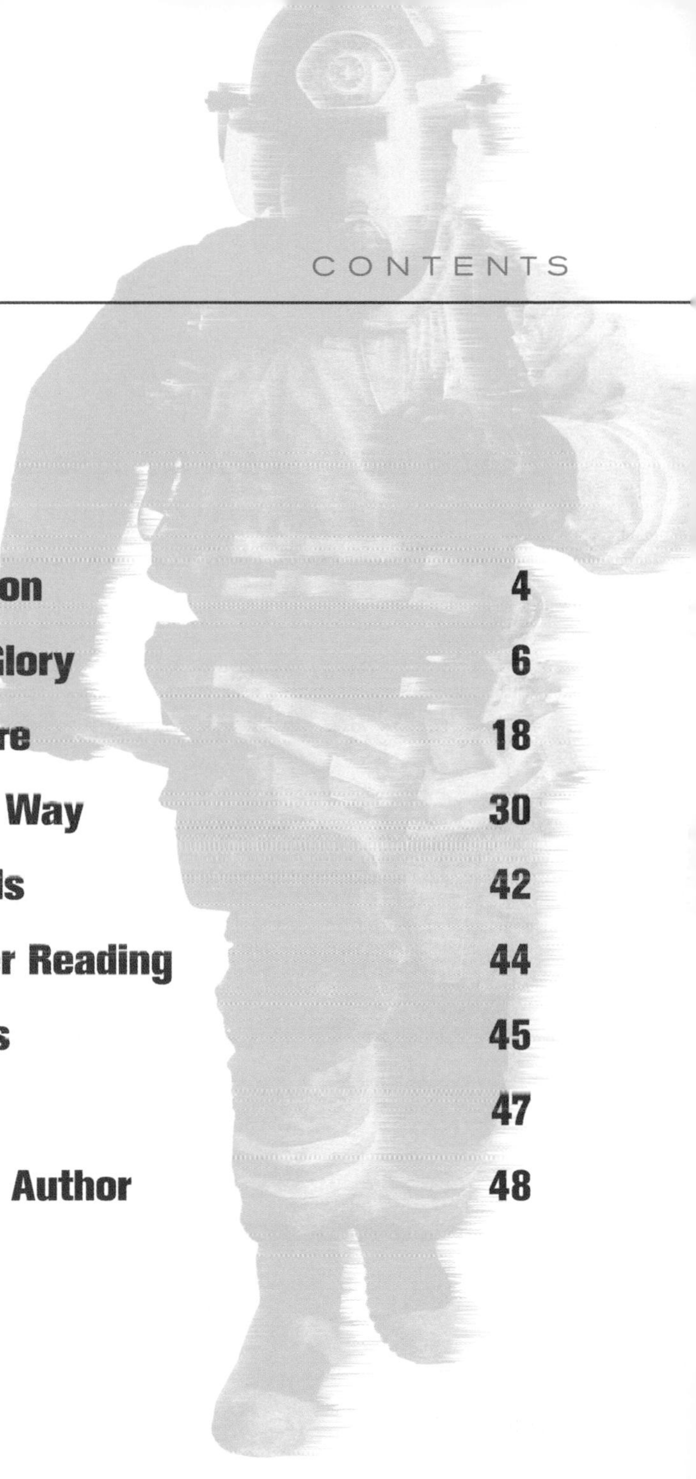

CONTENTS

Flames race through the insides of an apartment building. An elderly man is trapped on the fourth floor. He knows that he should not use an elevator in a burning building. However, he doesn't have the strength to run down the stairs. He is at his window, screaming for his life. Who will hear him? Who will help him?

A lone firefighter scrambles up a ladder that reaches the fourth floor. He ignores the closeness of the flames. He rushes past heat and ignores the ash that is falling around him. As the firefighter climbs, a fireball explodes on the floor below him. The windows shatter. Pieces of glass fly everywhere.

On the street below, other firefighters attach hoses to fire hydrants. When they are in position, they signal the other firefighters to turn on the water. The firefighters aim the water at the flames. Meanwhile, the firefighter above has reached the trapped man.

As the firefighter carries the man down, he hears a baby's cry. He spots a mother and her child at a second floor window. He shouts to the firefighters on the street,

Firefighters must be able to take the heat of any situation they face!

pointing to the trapped mother and baby. The fire worsens as more of the building burns. It's a race against time. Can the firefighters save everyone?

Being a firefighter requires courage, determination, and commitment. This book honors firefighters who stare down danger and death, day after day.

CHAPTER 1

Blaze of Glory

When fire is controlled, it becomes a vital tool. It gives light where there is darkness. It provides heat during the cold winter months. However, fire also has the potential for danger. One spark can set off a raging forest fire. A blaze can burn a whole city to the ground. Throughout history, firefighters have proudly served as our main line of defense from deadly fires.

Early Firefighters

The first organized fire fighting force was in ancient Rome. Emperor Augustus set up fire fighting teams made up of slaves and soldiers. These teams were called *vigiles*. Rome had close to seven thousand *vigiles*. *Vigiles* used pumps, ladders, and hooked poles to fight fire.

Fire is one of nature's most common – and destructive – forces. In 2001, fire departments in the United States responded to 1,734,500 fires. About 6,000 people lost their lives in these fires.

After the fall of Rome in the fourth century, the *vigiles* were no longer used. There was no other organized fire fighting force for several hundred years.

In the United States, organized fire fighting began in the 1600s. Volunteer firefighters combated fires by passing buckets of water to one another. The last person in the line would dump the bucket of water on the fire. These groups were usually called bucket brigades. In 1648, Peter Stuyvesant, the governor of New Amsterdam, made laws and regulations to prevent and fight fires in New Amsterdam. New Amsterdam would later become New York City. In 1736, Benjamin Franklin helped to form Philadelphia, Pennsylvania's first volunteer fire department. It was called the Union Fire Company. This led to the setting up of other fire departments in and around Philadelphia.

In the mid-1700s, the American colonies began to import fire pumps from Europe. Instead of using buckets, firefighters put out flames using steady streams of water from the pumps. Hand pumpers had

Most kinds of fire fighting equipment, such as ladders, hoses, and axes that were used in colonial times, are still used today.

long handles that the firefighters pumped up and down quickly to force the water out of the pumper's tank and onto the fire. At first, firefighters had to pull the pumps to the fire themselves. In the 1820s, however, horse-drawn pumps relieved overworked firefighters. Then, in the early 1900s, gasoline-powered

Today, firefighters depend on a city's water supply to fight fires. Connecting hoses to fire hydrants allow firefighters quick access to large amounts of water.

RISKY BUSINESS

In the early 1800s, the first cast-iron fire hydrant was used in Philadelphia, Pennsylvania. Hydrants draw water supplies from an underground system of pipes.

trucks replaced horsepower. Today, many fire departments have pumpers as well as tankers. Tankers can hold as much as 3,000 gallons of water. In large cities, firefighters get water from the city's water supply system through fire hydrants. Fire departments also use fire trucks that have ladders or platforms. Some fire truck ladders can extend to 100 feet or more.

Deadly Blazes

Firefighters push their bodies to the breaking point when they battle blazes. Some fires, though, are far too powerful to put out quickly. Here are a few of history's worst.

On the fortieth anniversary of the Great Chicago Fire, the Fire Marshals Association of North America established National Fire Prevention Day. This was done to make people more aware of the need for fire prevention.

The Great Chicago Fire

No one knows how this fire started. A legend traces the blaze's beginnings to a barn. The myth is that a Mrs. O'Leary had been milking her cow. Suddenly, the cow kicked over a nearby kerosene lamp. The lamp's flame then ignited the hay in the barn. This legend, though,

is unproven. What is known is that the fire began on Chicago's West Side on the evening of October 8, 1871. Strong winds helped the fire spread quickly.

Firefighters responded immediately. Unfortunately, they were sent to the wrong address. By the time they got to the right place, the fire was out of control.

It burned for two days before a rainstorm helped put it out. The blaze destroyed Chicago's main business area. Nearly three hundred people died in the fire. Another 100,000 were left homeless.

Triangle Shirtwaist Company Fire

On March 25, 1911, one of America's worst industrial fires occurred. It happened in a New York City clothing factory. The Triangle Shirtwaist Company was located on the eighth, ninth, and tenth floors of the Asch Building. After the fire started, workers ran for the exit, only to find the doors locked. The company's owners had ordered the doors locked to keep employees from leaving early. The workers were trapped.

Firefighters arrived to see people jumping from the windows. They took out their life nets. These nets were designed to catch people. Unfortunately, they were not made to withstand the force of people jumping from so high. About fifty people jumped 100 feet to their deaths. Firefighters desperately scrambled up ladders to try and reach the trapped workers. Unfortunately, their

The deadly effects of fire were shown in the
1911 Triangle Shirtwaist Company fire: In only
30 minutes, 146 people lost their lives.

ladders only reached the sixth floor. The blaze left 146 workers dead. Most of the workers were young girls.

It was later learned that the Asch Building had poor safety exits. Ladders connecting the levels of the fire escape were never installed. The public was angry about this tragic fire. Their anger led to changes in safety laws. Exits signs were expected to be clearly marked. More automatic sprinklers were installed in businesses. Fire drills were scheduled to teach workers what to do in case of a fire.

Fire on the Water

Fires don't have to happen in cities to destroy property and claim human lives. In fact, they don't even have to happen on dry land. Past midnight on September 8, 1934, a fire broke out on a passenger ship. The luxury ship *Morro Castle* was headed to New York, from Cuba. The ship had been equipped with fire doors and an alarm system—yet 137 people died in the fire. Why? There were many combustible objects and items on board. When something is combustible, it can easily burst into flame.

There were other mysteries surrounding the blaze. The fire may have been caused by arson. Arson is when a fire is started on purpose. Before the fire, the *Morro Castle*'s captain was found dead. First Mate William F. Warms took command. Warms, however, failed to send a call-for-help SOS signal immediately after the fire was discovered. Some suspect that Warms killed the captain and started the fire himself.

The Changing Role of Firefighters

While the destructive nature of fire has not changed, the role of the firefighter has. Today's firefighters do more than pass buckets of water to combat fires. They often have to handle hazardous materials and give expert medical assistance to people in need. Firefighters are often called to the scene of highway accidents. There, they use their skills and equipment to save the lives of many people.

CHAPTER 2

Trial by Fire

Several basic requirements must be met to become a firefighter in the United States. The minimum age to apply is usually eighteen or twenty-one years old. People who want to be firefighters must have clean criminal records. Also, they must agree to drug testing. They have to be in excellent physical and mental health. Applicants must have a high school diploma. Those without a high school diploma may get a General Equivalency Diploma (GED). A GED is similar to a high school diploma. There is a lot of competition to become a firefighter. To improve the chances of being picked, a person wanting to be a firefighter should have a college education.

Firefighters need to have many different skills, such as reading blueprints, to do their job the right way.

Testing

All firefighter candidates must take a written exam. This exam tests several skills including judgment, reasoning, and following directions. The ability to read and understand a map is another skill that is tested. For instance, a factory fire might require firefighters to use the building's blueprint, or floor plan, to locate sprinkler systems and fire exits. Blueprints may also be used to find windows quickly to allow poisonous smoke to escape the building.

Firefighters perform tough tasks in hostile surroundings. They must be strong and be able to endure a lot of stress—both physical and mental. They must be able to drag heavy firehoses. Firefighters need to have good balance. They climb ladders while holding heavy equipment. Also, they carry victims down stairs while moving through thick black smoke.

Once accepted into a fire department, candidates undergo weeks of serious training. They receive both classroom and hands-on instruction. They learn emergency medical procedures such as first aid and cardiopulmonary resuscitation (CPR). CPR is a medical procedure done to revive a person's heart and lungs. Candidates also study lifesaving fire fighting techniques. For instance, they learn how to prevent flashover. Flashover happens when the gases given off by a fire in an enclosed area, such as a room, becomes superheated and a fireball erupts.

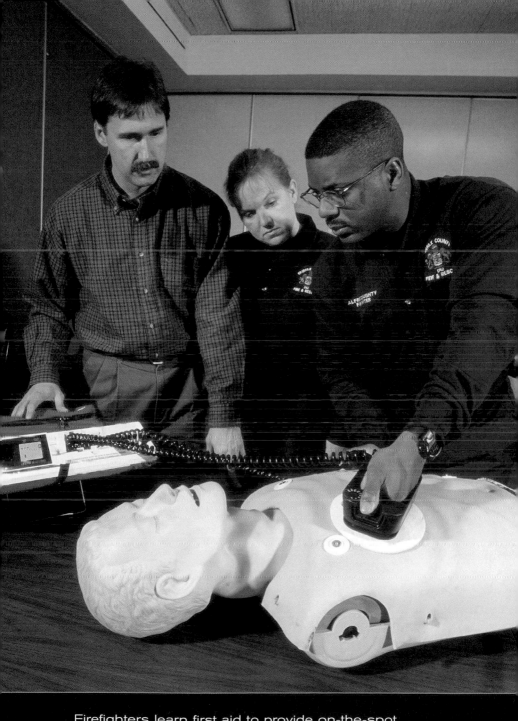

Firefighters learn first aid to provide on-the-spot emergency care.

Firefighters also learn to handle and control unsafe materials. For example, they may get called to put out a fire that started when a truck overturned. If the truck was carrying hazardous chemicals, the firefighters must proceed with caution. They need to know what kind of chemicals they're dealing with. How deadly are these chemicals? How long can the firefighters be near these chemicals before their health is affected?

Some departments have training programs for new firefighters. Basic training for new firefighters often takes about four months. However, firefighters sharpen their skills throughout their careers. After their basic training is complete, new firefighters are assigned to a firehouse.

Not Like Any Other Job

Firefighting is not a 9-to-5 job. Each fire department sets up its own work schedule. Some departments use 10-hour shifts. Others use a system of 24 hours on, 24 hours off. Firefighters work this way for three or four days. Then they get three or four days of rest.

RISKY BUSINESS

In times of emergency, such as a forest fire, firefighters might work without a break for several shifts.

A firefighter's workweek can be a tough one. They often work through holidays. They are responsible for protecting other families. Yet, they often don't get to see their own families for long stretches of time.

Firefighters must be able to think quickly under different conditions. They have to be able to cope with danger and fear. On the other hand, they must be able to relax when their job is over. If their stress level constantly remains high, their mental alertness will suffer. Firefighters must also have self-discipline, courage, and endurance. They must also have a strong sense of public service. After all, they put their lives at risk to save people they don't know.

While at work, many firefighters live in a firehouse with their coworkers. The firehouse becomes their second home. They do chores to keep the firehouse clean and working well. Also, between alarms, they inspect and maintain their trucks and equipment. These tasks help firefighters stay prepared. In many places, the fire department is made up of volunteer firefighters. These volunteers stop whatever they are doing when they are notified of a fire in progress and rush to the scene to offer help. Volunteer firefighters usually keep their fire fighting gear in their cars.

Death and Injury

Firefighters understand that their occupation comes with risks. Injuries and death are a part of the job. While flames can climb to intense temperatures, they're not always the most life-threatening element of a fire. Many firefighters die or receive their worst injuries from breathing in smoke. They can be overcome by smoke and may even choke to death on it.

In 2001, 439 firefighters died while on duty. The biggest single loss was the 340 firefighters who died in the September 11, 2001 terrorist attack on the World Trade Center in New York City.

Firefighters are also exposed to chemicals, gases, and other toxic substances. These dangerous vapors and liquids can have long-term effects on firefighters' health, such as serious difficulty in breathing.

Wherever Fire Strikes

Firefighters don't protect just cities and towns. Firefighters who battle wildfires in forests are called smoke jumpers. They are flown by airplane over a forest fire. They leap out of a plane and parachute toward the blaze. Smoke jumpers are trained to help contain the fire so that it doesn't spread. Once the fire is contained, it's easier to put out. Forest fires that aren't stopped can quickly burn and destroy thousands of acres of forests and wildlife.

Firefighters may use special fireboats to aid ships that are on fire. Airports also have specially trained firefighters. These firefighters are trained to handle airplane crashes and emergency landings. They use foam instead of water to contain and put out fires.

In the United States, forest fires are a constant problem. In 2002, there were over seventy thousand forest or wildland fires involving 7.1 million acres of land.

Dressed for Success

Firefighters wear fire-resistant coats and pants. These clothes are called Turnout gear. The gear provides protection from heat, cold, fire, and water. Firefighters also wear hoods to cover their heads. Hard helmets shield the firefighters from falling objects. Some helmets feature a face shield that keeps out heat,

SCBA

Flashlight

Protective Hood

PASS

A firefighter's Turnout gear will keep him or her safe from head to toe.

flame, and ash. Firefighters also use a Self-Contained Breathing Apparatus (SCBA). The SCBA provides them with fresh air. The SCBA includes a special mask that keeps smoke and heat away from a firefighter's face.

Firefighter Tools

To help them do their job better, firefighters use, wear, and carry the latest technological devices. These devices help safeguard firefighters' health. The Personal Alert Safety System (PASS) is small, but serves an important function. It alerts rescuers to the possibility of a downed or trapped firefighter. The PASS device has a motion sensor. It beeps if the firefighter wearing it hasn't moved in 30 seconds.

Hot Sights

One high-tech invention that's made a splash is the thermal-imaging camera. This amazing hand-held device is used to find fire victims inside smoke-filled and collapsed areas. The camera can actually find people by detecting their body heat. The device can also find fires hidden between walls, ceilings, or floors.

CHAPTER 3

In Harm's Way

A *firefighter's job is never done,* **thinks Timothy Moore as he scrubs the pots used to cook dinner. It's been a quiet shift—so far.**

Shattering the Quiet

In the afternoon, the fire crew got called to a restaurant on the town's east side. An elderly man had suffered a mild heart attack. The firefighters brought a portable defibrillator to the restaurant. They used this machine to get the man's heart beating normally again. The evening, though, has been uneventful. The hottest thing they've had to deal with tonight is their captain's chili. Moore's fellow firefighters are tending to after-dinner chores. Moore, of course, has dish duty.

Though not as exciting as fire fighting, maintaining equipment in the firehouse is very important.

The Company They Keep

Most fire departments have two basic fire fighting units. They are engine companies and ladder companies. Engine companies, like the one Moore belongs to, use trucks that have water pumps and hoses. Ladder companies use trucks with ladders of different lengths and an extending ladder or platform.

Suddenly, the wailing of the firehouse alarm interrupts Moore's pot scrubbing. The firefighters race to get into their Turnout gear. Moore slides into his gloves and boots. The boots are made to protect Moore from electrocution. By the time Moore finishes dressing, he's loaded down with 60 pounds of gear. With everyone on board, the fire engine roars out of the firehouse. On the truck, the firefighters put on their masks and tanks filled with compressed air. Sirens blare and the lights spin and flash. Neighbors stick their heads out of their windows to see where the trucks are headed.

On the Scene

Moore smells the fire before he sees it. The fire truck pulls up in front of an old four-story apartment building. Thick black smoke billows out of the windows. Flames flicker across the roof. The firefighters are on the move even before their trucks come to a complete stop. Hoses are attached to the nearest fire hydrant.

The frightened tenants are on the street. One man is in a bathrobe. He was taking a shower when the fire broke out. A woman is screaming uncontrollably. She's just returned to her home to see it burning. She knows her teenage daughter, Lourdes, is still in the building. Lourdes is trapped on the fourth floor, the source of the fire. The captain orders a pair of firefighters, Moore and Jorge Diego, into the building to find the girl.

Into the Fire

The inside of the building is dark and filled with smoke. The wooden steps of the staircase creak as Moore and Diego climb cautiously but quickly.

The apartment on fire is at the end of the hall. Moore takes out a tool called a Halligan. Using it, he pries open the apartment door. Moore dashes into the apartment. "Lourdes!" he yells. "Where are you?!" The girl does not respond. She may be so frightened that she can't speak. Moore knows that she may even be unconscious. Suddenly, the ceiling creaks and bulges. Moore and Diego know it will fall down soon.

Firefighters make a habit of climbing into danger to save people.

Firefighters never go into a fire without wearing their Personal Alert Safety System.

Moore and Diego call for backup on their radios. Their captain sends up a second pair of firefighters, Chris Gold and Rachel Mitchell. Mitchell tears a hole through one of the apartment walls. This gives them another escape route besides the door.

Finally, Moore finds the girl in the bedroom. She is huddled in the closet, shaking with fear. Moore grabs her and heads out. Gold and Diego are using the hose to put out as much of the fire in the apartment as possible.

Suddenly, a piece of the weakening roof collapses. Moore does his best to shield the girl from the falling rubble. Debris and flaming embers rain down upon him. Hunks of concrete pound his back. He uses his body to shield the girl from the falling concrete chunks. They are both trapped.

After 30 seconds of him lying still, his PASS monitor begins to beep. His fellow firefighters hear the beeping. Gold and Mitchell rush to his aid. They pull Moore and the girl from the rubble. Moore and Gold take the girl downstairs. Diego continues dousing the apartment. He can barely see through the blanket of smoke.

Moore, Gold, and the girl reach the lobby and leave the building. Meanwhile, on the fourth floor, the fire continues to spread. Suddenly, it's not just the kitchen that's burning. The couch in the living room is on fire. The drapes by Lourdes's bedroom window have also caught fire. Diego and Mitchell rush down the stairs. Just as they get outside, a huge fireball explodes in the building's entrance. Large sections of the roof collapse. Diego suffers severe burns and injuries from flying debris.

No Time for Tears

Several hours later, Moore wakes up in the hospital. He has a concussion, bruised ribs, and a sprained back. Fortunately, Lourdes was not seriously injured. A quick investigation had revealed that the fire started in the kitchen. Lourdes had been cooking dinner. A kitchen towel left near the stove caught fire. With one spark, a simple meal became a major disaster.

Reuniting a parent with a child is one of the best rewards for a firefighter.

The next morning, Moore hears some terrible news. Diego has died from the injuries he got when the building collapsed. Diego was one of the department's best firefighters. He was also one of Moore's closest friends.

A week later, Moore joins the rest of his department at a memorial service for Diego. Firefighters from across the country attend the service. Diego's wife and two young children are there, so is his father, a retired fire captain. Many firefighters follow in the footsteps of family members. Sometimes, generation after generation of a single family will choose this life of danger.

Moore returns to the firehouse. There are things to do. Equipment has to be checked and reports still need to be written. Moore sits by himself. "I can't do this again," he says, softly. "That could have been me who died." A chill runs up his aching back. The blaring of the fire alarm interrupts his thoughts. Moore shuts his eyes. His training kicks in. He springs into action, putting on his Turnout gear and jumping onto the fire truck. Once again, he's not afraid of the risk. Somewhere, people are in trouble. He will do his best to help them, no matter what the danger. A firefighter's job is never done.

arson (**ar**-suhn) the deliberate burning of
something that is meant to cause harm

brigades (bri-**gaydz**) organized groups of workers

cardiopulmonary resuscitation (CPR)
(kar-dee-oh-**pul**-muh-ner-ee ri-sus-uh-**tay**-shuhn)
an emergency procedure for reviving the heart
and lungs

combustible (kuhm-**buhss**-tuh-buhl) capable of
catching fire and burning

compressed air (kuhm-**pressed air**) air under
pressure greater than that of the atmosphere

defibrillator (dee-**fih**-bruh-lay-tuhr) a device that
applies electric shock to the heart

Halligan (**hal**-uh-guhn) a tool used for prying
windows and doors open

hazardous (**haz**-ur-duhss) dangerous or risky

procedures (pruh-**see**-jurz) ways of doing things, especially by a series of steps

smoke jumpers (**smohk juhm**-purz) firefighters who are flown over forest fires and dropped off

thermal-imaging camera (**thur**-muhl **im**-ih-jing **kam**-ur-uh) a device used to find trapped or buried victims and hidden fires within walls and ceilings

Turnout gear (**turn**-out **gihr**) the protective clothing that firefighters wear

vigiles (vi-**juhlz**) the first group of firefighters that was created by the Roman emperor Augustus

Faith, Nicholas. *Blaze: The Forensics of Fire.* New York: St. Martin's Press, 2000.

Goldberg, Jan. *Fire Fighter.* Mankato, MN: Capstone Press, 1999.

Golway, Terry. *So Others Might Live.* New York: Basic Books, 2002.

Gottschalk, Jack. *Firefighting.* New York: DK Publishing, Inc., 2002.

Smith, Dennis. *Firefighters: Their Lives in Their Own Words.* New York: Broadway Books, 2002.

Smith, Dennis. *Report from Ground Zero: The Story of the Rescue Efforts at the World Trade Center.* New York: Viking, 2002.

Organizations
United States Fire Administration
16825 South Seton Avenue
Emmitsburg, MD 21727
(301) 447-1000

National Volunteer Fire Council
1050 17th Street, NW, Suite 490
Washington, DC 20036
(202) 887-5700

Web Sites
The Phoenix Fire Department
www.ci.phoenix.az.us/FIRE
This is the official Web site of the Fire
Department of Phoenix, Arizona.

Firehouse.com

www.firehouse.com

This site offers articles about fire fighting history and techniques. Many are written by professional firefighters.

New York City Fire Museum

www.nycfiremuseum.org

This is the official Web site of the New York City Fire Department Museum. It offers a history of fire fighting in New York City.

About the Author

Philip Abraham is a freelance writer. He has written many books for children and young adults.